This

Bible Story Time book

belongs to

_____

_____

_____

Text by Sophie Piper
Illustrations copyright © 2006 Estelle Corke
This edition copyright © 2014 Lion Hudson

Published by Lion Children's Books
an imprint of
Lion Hudson plc
Wilkinson House, Jordan Hill Road,
Oxford OX2 8DR, England
www.lionhudson.com/lionchildrens

ISBN 978 0 7459 6365 5
e-ISBN 978 0 7459 6818 6

First edition 2006
This edition 2014

A catalogue record for this book is available from the British Library

Printed and bound in China, October 2013, LH06

Bible Story Time

The Lost Sheep

Sophie Piper ✳ Estelle Corke

LION
CHILDREN'S

One day, a crowd of people came to listen to Jesus.

There were all kinds of people.

Some were rich. Some were poor.

Some always obeyed the law.

Some were always in trouble.

6

The Lost Sheep

Some of the people were rather proud of themselves.

"Do you know what annoys me about coming to see Jesus?" whispered one of them. "We always end up sitting close to the wrong kind of person."

"I know," answered another.
"Jesus seems to like them. It makes
me wonder – perhaps he's the
wrong kind of person too."

Jesus knew what they were thinking.
He started telling a story.
 "There was once a man who had
100 sheep.

"He counted his sheep every evening, as he let them run into the sheepfold.

"'Stay inside,' he used to say to them. 'I don't want any wild animals to steal you away.

"'If any come near, I'll be here to scare them off.'

"He counted his sheep every morning, when he led them out of the sheepfold.

"'Come on,' he used to say. 'We must go down to the stream where you can drink.'

"He counted his sheep in the daytime, as they nibbled the green grass.

"'Bother,' he said one day. 'I think I got the numbers muddled.

" 'I only counted to 99. I'm going to count again.'

"He counted very carefully. To his dismay, there were only 99 sheep left.

" 'Oh dear,' he said. He picked up his shepherd's stick.

" 'I'm going to have to go and find my lost sheep.'

"He left the green fields and went up into the hills. He looked among the rocks. He looked among the thorn bushes.

"He looked everywhere.

"At last he found his lost sheep.
He was overjoyed.

"He picked it up and carried it
back to the flock.

"As he came home that day,
he called out to his friends.

"'Look! This is the sheep I lost.
I found it.

"'Come round to my house
tonight. I'm going to have
a party.'"

Jesus looked at the proud people. He looked at the people who always seemed to be in trouble.

"God is like that shepherd," said Jesus. "God cares about the people who get things wrong. God goes looking for them, so they can be part of God's family again."

When that happens, the angels in heaven are as happy as can be.